This journal belongs to

_____

God's splendor is a tale that is told.

PSALM 19:1 TPT

Belle City Gifts
Racine, Wisconsin, USA

Belle City Gifts is an imprint of BroadStreet Publishing Group LLC.
Broadstreetpublishing.com

God's Splendor Is a Tale that Is Told
Travel Journal

© 2015 by BroadStreet Publishing

ISBN 978-1-4245-5071-5 (hard cover)

Unless otherwise noted, stories and quotations composed by Vicki Kuyper.

Design by Chris Garborg | www.garborgdesign.com
Compiled and edited by Michelle Winger | www.literallyprecise.com

Printed in China.

15 16 17 18 19 20 21   7 6 5 4 3 2 1

I will instruct you and teach you
in the way you should go;
I will counsel you with
my eye upon you.

Psalm 32:8 ESV

LOOK AGAIN

*O*ur world is so big that even if we traveled every day of our lives we'd never see it all. There would still be lagoons to snorkel, mountains to crest, and hidden nooks and crannies of creation to explore. Earth is merely a grain of sand on the shore of a limitless universe.

And still we get bored. We simply stop exploring because we believe we've already conquered this tiny corner of the universe. But right under our noses there are buds beginning to bloom, leaves preparing to fall, lizards scurrying over rocks, or tiny ants carrying tremendous loads. Above us there's a sky filled with so many distant worlds that our minds cannot fathom its expanse.

Today, wherever the road takes you, open your eyes. Instead of hurrying past what you've already seen, look again. Take time to appreciate the detail God has woven into nature. Look at the faces of the people you pass along the street. Notice the buildings, the food, the artwork, the amazing innovation, and the imagination that originated from the human brain—another of God's masterworks.

The God of gods, the mighty Lord himself, has spoken!
He shouts out over all the people of the earth,
In every brilliant sunrise and every beautiful sunset,
saying, "Listen to me!"

Psalm 50:1 TPT

....
....
....
....
....
....
....
....
....
....
....
....
....
....
....
....
....
....

Learning is not at odds with relaxation. It can spark new
interests, challenge us to rethink long-held opinions,
and stir up some interesting conversations.

Be still, and know that I am God;

I will be exalted among the nations,

I will be exalted in the earth!

Psalm 46:10 NKJV

Happy memories are a great souvenir.
They're free, easy to carry, and never need dusting.

*L*et the sea and everything in it shout his praise!
Let the earth and all living things join in.

Psalm 98:7 NLT

On vacation days, we often experience situations that will put our patience, preconceived notions, and unconditional love to the test. These days provide the perfect petri dish in which faith can grow!

I lie awake at night thinking of you—of how much you have helped me—and how I rejoice through the night beneath the protecting shadow of your wings.

Psalm 63:6-7 TLB

There's no better time than today to begin a practice of quietness that helps us enjoy the beauty of the moment and invites us to draw closer to God at the same time.

Don't be pulled in different directions or worried about a thing. Be saturated in prayer throughout each day, offering your faith-filled requests before God with overflowing gratitude. Tell him every detail of your life.

Philippians 4:6 TPT

To be a Christian without prayer is no more possible than
to be alive without breathing.

–Martin Luther

15

*T*he earth is the LORD'S, and everything in it,

the world, and all who live in it.

Psalm 24:1 NIV

God designed us for relationship;

we are children created to love and be loved.

We can make our plans,
but the final outcome is in God's hands.

Proverbs 16:1 TLB

We may believe the purpose of our vacation is to see the
world, but God may have an even richer purpose in mind.

With the completion of Route 66 in the summer of 1926, the road trip was born. Kitschy motels, roadside diners, and miles of open highway enticed travelers to drive from Chicago all the way to the California coast. Though only portions of the Mother Road remain, road trips are still going strong. They're one of the most affordable kinds of travel, especially for families. Spending long hours together buckled into a moving vehicle gives new meaning to the words *captive audience*.

In the heyday of Route 66, people spent most of their time on the road enjoying the view out the window and carrying on a conversation with their fellow travelers. Back then, the idea that children would watch movies, play video games, or wear headphones so they could listen to their own music, while parents talked on their phones, would have sounded like a space-age fantasy. That fantasy is our present-day reality.

While it's true that the gadgets and gizmos we use on the road can help pass the time, they do nothing to draw a family closer together. And isn't that what a vacation is all about? There will never come a day when we look back on a family vacation and lament, "I wish we'd spent more time playing video games." But there will come a time when we'll long for just one more moment with the ones we love. Make the most of those moments today.

21

On the seventh day God had finished his work of creation,
so he rested from all his work.

Genesis 2:2 NLT

_____

_____

_____

_____

_____

_____

_____

_____

_____

_____

_____

_____

_____

_____

_____

_____

Play time is as important for adults as it is for kids. We need
time to laugh, to explore, to create, to try new things, to
dream. We need to give ourselves permission to allow the
child in us to come out and play.

Then you will go on your way in safety,
and your foot will not stumble.
When you lie down, you will not be afraid;
when you lie down, your sleep will be sweet.

Proverbs 3:23-24 NIV

....
....
....
....
....
....
....
....
....
....
....
....
....
....
....
....

_____

_____

_____

_____

_____

_____

_____

_____

_____

_____

_____

_____

_____

_____

_____

Travel can weave a crazy quilt of emotions inside us.
The one that should overwhelm us again and again is gratitude.

*T*he steadfast love of
the Lord never ceases;
his mercies never come to an end;
they are new every morning;
great is your faithfulness.

Lamentations 3:22-23 ESV

....
....
....
....
....
....
....
....
....
....
....
....
....
....
....
....

Having enough to eat—or more than enough—is not a given.
It is a gift. Taking time to thank God for what's on our plate—
whether it's samosas, kimchi, or pickled pigs' feet—reminds us
that food is first and foremost fuel. Taste is an added bonus.

*Y*ou saw me before I was born.
Every day of my life was recorded in your book.
Every moment was laid out
before a single day had passed.

Psalm 139:16 NLT

....
....
....
....
....
....
....
....
....
....
....
....
....
....

Happy memories are an irreplaceable gift.

"*S*top and consider
the wondrous works of God."

Job 37:14, ESV

We travel not to escape life, but for life not to escape us.

−Anonymous

I say to myself, "If only I could fly away from all of this!
If only I could run away to the place of rest and peace.
I would run far away where no one could find me,
Escaping to a wilderness retreat."

Psalm 55:6-7 TPT

....

....

....

....

....

....

....

....

....

....

....

....

....

....

....

....

....

How beautiful it is to do nothing and then rest afterwards.

When we obey him, every path he guides us on is
fragrant with his loving-kindness and his truth.

Psalm 25:10 TLB

Wherever today finds you, you're surrounded by God's
handiwork. Every landscape, every wildflower, every face
that you see can remind you of him—and provide a clue
about the character of his divine nature.

BETWEEN HEAVEN AND THE DEEP BLUE SEA

*N*ot every journey leads to the sea, but with the ocean covering more than 70% of our planet, chances are good that we'll fly over it, sail on it, dive beneath it, or lounge beside it at least once during our lifetime. And even once is enough to leave a permanent impression.

Its moods are as profound as its mystery. One minute it's as calm as a shallow pond. The next, its surface roils like water in a teakettle, set to boil. Waves crash and tides turn, casting briny treasures up onto the shore. Seashells, starfish, and clumps of kelp provide just a glimpse of what lies beneath—evidence of a fantastically foreign world.

In some ways, the ocean is a bit like heaven. It's as close as our last breath, but it's impossible for us to explore without undergoing a physical change. It's a foreign land and our true home at the same time. Certainly our limited language can't help but fail when it comes to accurately describing a world where God dwells in all his glory. Like the deepest depths of the sea, heaven's borders are beyond our grasp right now.

Listen to the waves, take deep breaths of the salty sea air, and pick up a shell along the shore. Allow the ocean to become a touchstone to heaven for you—a reminder that there's so much more to this life than what we can see with our eyes.

*T*his is the day the LORD has made;

We will rejoice and be glad in it.

Psalm 118:24 NKJV

It's no use to grumble and complain; it's just as cheap and easy to rejoice; when God sorts out the weather and sends rain—why, rain's my choice.

–JAMES WHITCOMB RILEY

Whether you eat or drink or whatever you do,
do it all for the glory of God.

1 Corinthians 10:31 NIV

If we have the ability to travel for pleasure, we are privileged—
even if our lodgings are solely economy and our meals are
ordered at a drive-thru window. Any vacation we take is a gift.
Let's open it with gratitude and enjoy it to the fullest.

I remember what happened long ago;
I consider everything you have done.
I think about all you have made.

Psalm 143:5 NCV

You are never too old to set another goal
or dream a new dream.

–C.S. Lewis

Warn those who are lazy, comfort those who are frightened, take tender care of those who are weak, and be patient with everyone. See that no one pays back evil for evil, but always try to do good to each other and to everyone else.

1 Thessalonians 5:14–15 TLB

Do all the good you can, by all the means you can, in all the
ways you can, in all the places you can, at all the times you can,
to all the people you can, as long as ever you can.

–JOHN WESLEY

45

Ever since the world was created, people have seen the earth and sky. Through everything God made, they can clearly see his invisible qualities—his eternal power and divine nature. So they have no excuse for not knowing God.

Romans 1:20 NLT

Every person in a crowd is a story being written
one moment at a time.

Our citizenship is in heaven.

Philippians 3:20 NIV

By choosing to super-size our love and travel-size our possessions, we can make the most of the time we have here on earth and leave behind a legacy of incomparable worth.

"Take your sandals off your feet, for the place on which you are standing is holy ground."

Exodus 3:5 ESV

_____

_____

_____

_____

_____

_____

_____

_____

_____

_____

_____

_____

_____

We may never see a burning bush in Central Park, but we may
become more aware of God's whisper when the wind blows through
the trees over our heads, or of God's loving care for all he's made
when we delight in a blanket of wildflowers beneath our feet. The
more aware we are of God's presence with us at all times, the more
tempted we may be to take off our shoes.

We should love people not only with words and talk, but by our actions and true caring.

1 John 3:18 NCV

....
....
....
....
....
....
....
....
....
....
....
....
....
....
....
....
....

Making friends while we're making memories—
even if we never understand a word the other person says—
makes every journey a more enjoyable one.

53

DIVINE
TREASURE HUNT

What are we looking for when we're on vacation? Adventure? Beauty? Knowledge? Relaxation? Perhaps one of the things our heart is actually searching for is God. We're looking for evidence of his power in the ferocity of the sea, his tenderness in the delicate dance of the clouds, and a faint shadow of his image in the faces of those whose culture and life experience are literally a world apart from our own.

This isn't a futile search. Scripture tells us God has left divine fingerprints on everything he's made. God's world is like a treasure map pointing us right back to him. All we have to do is follow the clues.

As we travel through the world God's made, one way for us to uncover more about the Creator's character is to invite him along. Of course, he's always with us wherever we go, whether we invite him or not. Acknowledging him reminds us to look for signs of his power and clues to his character as we head out to partake of whatever adventure we've planned for the day.

Like cold water to a weary soul
is good news from a distant land.

Proverbs 25:25 NIV

....

....

....

....

....

....

....

....

....

....

....

....

....

....

....

....

....

....

What if the point of our travels is not in seeing how the world
changes *us*, but in how our presence changes *the world*?

"*I* am leaving you with a gift—peace of mind and heart. And the peace I give is a gift the world cannot give. So don't be troubled or afraid."

John 14:27 NLT

God cannot give us happiness and peace apart from Himself
because it is not there. There is no such thing.

—C.S. Lewis

Blessed are those whose strength is in you,
whose hearts are set on pilgrimage.

Psalm 84:5 NIV

....

....

....

....

....

....

....

....

....

....

....

....

....

....

....

If all the world is sacred—because there's not a corner
where God's presence isn't found—then any journey can
be a pilgrimage and every traveler a pilgrim.

You see me when I travel and when I rest at home.
You know everything I do.

Psalm 139:3 NLT

Delight in every unexpected joy God brings your way.

*L*et all that I am praise the LORD;
may I never forget the good things he does for me.

Psalm 103:2 NLT

Let's do more than count our blessings. Let's make our blessings count. The more we take time to celebrate the gifts we've been given, the more grateful we'll feel.

"*D*o not fear, for I am with you;
Do not anxiously look about you, for I am your God.
I will strengthen you, surely I will help you,
Surely I will uphold you with My righteous right hand."

Isaiah 41:10 NASB

To reconnect with God, you first have to disconnect—
turn off your phone and power down your computer.
Plug yourself into the ultimate power source. It's a
great way to recharge from the inside out.

*Those who live in the shelter of the Most High
will find rest in the shadow of the Almighty.
This I declare about the LORD:
He alone is my refuge, my place of safety;
he is my God, and I trust him.*

Psalm 91:1-2 NLT

The more aware we are of God's presence wherever we go, the more opportunities for growth we'll find open up to us along the way.

The Lord will keep you from all harm—
he will watch over your life;
the Lord will watch over your coming and going
both now and forevermore.

Psalm 121:7-8 NIV

We can find great joy in the nostalgia of what's familiar,
but we need to add to our store of memories
and not try to survive on a life of reruns.

The heavens are yours; the earth also is yours;
the world and all that is in it, you have founded them.

Psalm 89:11 ESV

It's better to see something once than
to hear about it a thousand times.

—Anonymous

EXPLORING GOD'S GALLERY

*P*aris, Barcelona, Istanbul, NYC: sometimes we travel to experience a slice of civilization that's unlike our own. Other times, we're drawn to solitary, uncivilized places. Destinations where the only art gallery is the great outdoors—each masterwork signed by the hand of God.

For those of us who know the artist personally, spending time in God's gallery can draw us closer to him. But even those who haven't yet made his acquaintance acknowledge that there's something powerful about nature. It evokes a sense of awe that bears a keen resemblance to worship even in those who aren't certain who or what they are worshipping.

Let awe find a permanent home in your heart. Experience some of God's amazing creations firsthand. When your vacation is over, continue to nurture a sense of wonder and delight in creation. Even if you can't see the Grand Canyon every day, you can look in the mirror. The Bible tells us that's where God's greatest masterpiece can be found.

"*I* am the one who made the earth
and created people to live on it.
With my hands I stretched out the heavens.
All the stars are at my command."

Isaiah 45:12 NLT

The real voyage of discovery consists not in seeking
new landscapes, but in having new eyes.

−MARCEL PROUST

"With my great strength and powerful arm I made the earth and all its people and every animal. I can give these things of mine to anyone I choose."

Jeremiah 27:5 NLT

Travel is the only thing you buy that makes you richer.

—Anonymous

"You are worthy, our Lord and God, to receive glory and honor and power, for you created all things, and by your will they were created and have their being."

Revelation 4:11 NIV

The world is not a checklist of things to see and do that
we can cross off in one lifetime. It's a curiosity shop, so
filled with mysterious treasures that every time we take
another look, we discover something new.

Who has measured the waters in the hollow of his hand and marked off the heavens with a span, enclosed the dust of the earth in a measure and weighed the mountains in scales and the hills in a balance?

Isaiah 40:12 ESV

You can't see the whole sky through a bamboo tube.

—JAPANESE SAYING

*P*raise him, sun and moon;
praise him, all you shining stars.
Praise him, you highest heavens
and you waters above the skies.

Psalm 148:3-5 NIV

Return to your favorite place,
but don't forget to pack a fresh point of view.

Who gives the sun for light by day
And the fixed order of the moon and the stars for light by night,
Who stirs up the sea so that its waves roar;
The LORD of hosts is His name.

Jeremiah 31:35 NASB

Travel broadens the mind.

—Anonymous

He himself gives everyone life and breath and everything else. From one man he made all the nations, that they should inhabit the whole earth; and he marked out their appointed times in history and the boundaries of their lands.... He is not far from any one of us. For in him we live and move and have our being.

Acts 17:25-28 NIV

Do not let your happiness depend
on something you may lose.

–C.S. Lewis

Through him all things were made; without him
nothing was made that has been made.

John 1:3 NIV

Unless we learn to cherish *home*, and the beauty of an ordinary day, we may wind up believing that the best part of life is our next big trip to somewhere else. If we do, we'll miss what's right in front of us: the adventure waiting at our own front door.

For the life of every living thing is in his hand,
and the breath of every human being.

Job 12:10 NLT

No exotic location could ever provide the joy we find
in the presence of those we love.

SUNRISE, SUNSET

*L*eave it to an artist to begin and end each day with a masterpiece. At sunrise and sunset, God paints the sky with color, light, and creativity. Some days carry a more subtle light show than others, but all are worthy of notice. Each momentary display happens only once in the history of time.

The fact that the sun rises and sets every single day lulls us into the mistaken belief that nothing extraordinary is taking place. Unless the entire sky looks like a raging wildfire, we rarely stop what we're doing and take note. Even then, we may snap a quick photo to post online or admire later instead of enjoying it here and now.

Vacations are different. We break our routine. We expect to see and do things that are out of the ordinary. So why not make time to enjoy sunrises and sunsets? Why not choose one morning to wake before dawn and witness the first light of day? Or sit quietly with God and watch his light show from beginning to end in the evening? Tell him what you think of his handiwork. You may find those few quiet moments of contemplation and praise are the highlight of your day.

95

Let the heavens be glad, and the earth rejoice!
Let the sea and everything in it shout his praise!
Let the fields and their crops burst out with joy!
Let the trees of the forest rustle with praise before the LORD,

for he is coming!

Psalm 96:11-13 NLT

For in the true nature of things, if we rightly consider, every green tree is far more glorious than if it were made of gold and silver.

–MARTIN LUTHER

In whose hand are the depths of the earth,

The peaks of the mountains are His also.

The sea is His, for it was He who made it,

And His hands formed the dry land.

Come, let us worship and bow down,

Let us kneel before the LORD our Maker.

Psalm 95:4-6 NASB

....

....

....

....

....

....

....

....

....

....

....

....

....

....

....

....

If the visible world is so immense and complex that we can never
fully comprehend it, surely the invisible world is even more so.

*L*ORD, you have made many things;
with your wisdom you made them all.
The earth is full of your riches.
Look at the sea, so big and wide,
with creatures large and small that cannot be counted.

Psalm 104:24-25 NCV

A vacation is not just a destination. It includes a journey.
We can't travel without moving!

He loves righteousness and justice;
The earth is full of the goodness of the Lᴏʀᴅ.

Psalm 33:5 ɴᴋᴊᴠ

When our vacation is centered around the people we love, what we do and where we go doesn't matter as much. Love can be tricky and messy, but it can also be the deepest, richest part of our lives.

God has given them a desire to know the future.
He does everything just right and on time, but people can never
completely understand what he is doing.

Ecclesiastes 3:11 NCV

Expect the best, pack for the worst, and prepare to make
some unexpected memories along the way.

"*For* you shall go out in joy,
and be led back in peace;
the mountains and the hills before you
shall burst into song,
and all the trees of the field shall clap their hands."

Isaiah 55:12 NRSV

It is good to have an end to journey toward; but it is the
journey that matters, in the end.

–ERNEST HEMINGWAY

" You alone are the Lord. You made the heavens, even the highest heavens, and all their starry host, the earth and all that is on it, the seas and all that is in them. You give life to everything, and the multitudes of heaven worship you."

Nehemiah 9:6 NIV

_____

_____

_____

_____

_____

_____

_____

_____

_____

_____

_____

_____

_____

_____

Imagine every image you take as a thank-you postcard to
God. Not only will you find a unique way to spend more time
interacting with your heavenly Father, you'll also find your
inner well of gratitude overflowing more regularly.

GO AHEAD
AND GIGGLE

*P*ray for a sense of humor on your vacation. You know you're going to need it somewhere along the way. Your suitcase is going to take an unexpected trip around the world without you. The special Jacuzzi tub in your room is going to misfire, providing an unscheduled performance of dancing waters. The unpronounceable entree you order will be so spicy you'll cry harder than you did at your daughter's wedding. Or customer service will be so laughably lacking you'll find yourself searching for a hidden camera.

Regardless of the situation, getting giddy beats getting frustrated every time. It helps us see things from a more positive perspective. It also benefits us physically. Laughter boosts our energy, strengthens our immune system, releases endorphins, and reduces stress. It's one of the best workouts we can find without going anywhere near the gym.

Let's take our vacations, and ourselves, a little less seriously. The vacation time we've set aside isn't a critical task we're required to accomplish. It's a gift to be opened leisurely and enjoyed. By asking God to help us keep our sense of humor close at hand throughout our holiday, we'll not only have a better time, we'll have much more enjoyable stories to share with others when we return.

*L*ong ago you laid the foundation of the earth
and made the heavens with your hands.

Psalm 102:25 NLT

Stay curious: keep asking questions, exploring new places, and being humbled by the fact that there's always more to learn.

The LORD is my shepherd; I shall not want.

He makes me lie down in green pastures.

He leads me beside still waters.

He restores my soul.

Psalm 23:2-3 ESV

Travel can challenge and delight us. It can open our eyes,
stretch our minds, and charm our hearts. But it can also
make us appreciate the quiet pleasures of home.

When I consider your heavens,
the work of your fingers,
the moon and the stars,
which you have set in place,
what is mankind that you are mindful of them,
human beings that you care for them?

Psalm 8:3-4 NIV

Just say no to boredom. Nurture curiosity instead of apathy.

You don't have to stop exploring—

even if you never journey far from home.

The LORD directs the steps of the godly.
He delights in every detail of their lives.

Psalm 37:23 NLT

Choosing to use free time in a way that refreshes the soul is a wise choice. Let's just be certain it's still a choice and not a habit.

Trust in the LORD with all your heart;
do not depend on your own understanding.
Seek his will in all you do,
and he will show you which path to take.

Proverbs 3:5-6 NLT

Life is a journey that keeps moving forward.

" *Y*ours, O LORD, is the greatness and the power and the glory and the victory and the majesty, for all that is in the heavens and in the earth is yours.... Both riches and honor come from you, and you rule over all. In your hand are power and might, and in your hand it is to make great and to give strength to all.

1 Chronicles 29:11-12 ESV

Whether we're on the road, or safe at home, putting God's will before our own reminds us who is actually in control at all times.

"My Presence will go with you, and I will give you rest."

Exodus 33: 14 NIV

_____
_____
_____
_____
_____
_____
_____
_____
_____
_____
_____
_____
_____
_____
_____
_____
_____
_____

Listen for what God has to say to you in the spaces between
activities, when you're quiet enough to hear his voice.

"*I* will never fail you. I will never abandon you."

Hebrews 13:5 NLT

From the miracle of birth to the laws of gravity,
the world God created is wonder piled upon wonder.

The LORD is near to all who call upon Him,
To all who call upon Him in truth.

Psalm 145:18 NKJV

Make the most of the time spent in the company of those you love. They are always worth the journey.

"*H*is purpose was for the nations to seek after God and perhaps feel their way toward him and find him— though he is not far from any one of us."

Acts 17:27 NLT

Jesus is God spelling himself out in language
humanity can understand.

–S.D. Gordon

131

"The LORD your God is with you;
the mighty One will save you.
He will rejoice over you.
You will rest in his love;
he will sing and be joyful about you."

Zephaniah 3:17 NCV

Asking God to join us on our journey helps make us more
aware of his presence at every turn.

*Y*our word is like a lamp for my feet
and a light for my path.

Psalm 119:105 NCV

At heart, each and every one of us is a lost pilgrim searching for the road home. We're all in need of a knowledgeable guide to help us navigate the twists and turns of life.

These commandments that I give you today are to be on your hearts....
Talk about them when you sit at home and when you walk along the
road, when you lie down and when you get up.

Deuteronomy 6:6-7 NIV

Wherever we go, we go with God. May every journey you take, and memory you make, help you become more aware of his power, his presence, and his love.

All great vacations must come to an end. And we're fully aware of what's waiting for us when we get home. But we're not home yet. One of the biggest challenges we have as our vacation draws to a close is to prevent our minds from heading home before our bodies do. Whether we have a day, an afternoon, or even an hour of vacation left, let's not waste it. Why let tomorrow rob us of the pleasure and opportunities of today?

While *carpe diem* has become a modern day catch phrase, *carpe cras* has not. Sure, it doesn't sound as melodic, but more importantly, it can't be done. *Carpe cras* means "seize tomorrow." No matter how hard we try, we can't reach that far. Besides, none of us knows for certain what tomorrow will bring. Carrying the stress and worry of something that isn't here yet, or may never happen, can be amazingly taxing. Let's refuse to pick it up in the first place. Instead, let's grab hold of here and now and savor every moment.